How Does Earth's Surface Change?

Houghton Mifflin Harcourt™

PHOTOGRAPHY CREDITS: COVER (bg) ©Stan Rohrer/Alamy Images; 3 (b) ©Dennis Albert Richardson/Shutterstock; 4 (t) ©Stan Rohrer/Alamy Images; 5 (b) ©David Wall Photography/Lonely Planet Images/Getty Images; 6 (b) Photodisc/Getty Images; 7 (r) ©Corbis; 8 (t) ©Getty Images; 9 (bg) Dusty Pixel Photography/FlickrGetty Images; 10 (b) ©Bjorn Holland/The Image Bank/Getty Images; 12 (b) ©Kenneth Garrett/National Geographic/Getty Images; 13 (t) ©ribeiroantonio/Shutterstock; 14 (t) ©Jo Ingate/Alamy Images; 15 (t) ©Siede Preis/Photodisc/Getty Images; 16 (l) ©Marcio Jose Bastos Silva/Shutterstock; 16 (r) ©Purestock/Getty Images; 17 (r) ©John Warburton-Lee/AWL Images/Getty Images; 19 (b) ©Chris Saulit/Flickr/Getty Images; 21 (r) © H. David Seawell/Corbis

Printed in China

ISBN: 978-0-544-07352-4

19 20 21 0940 20 19 18

4500744966   B C D E F

Be an Active Reader!

Look at these words.

weathering	fossil	index fossil
erosion	mold	mass extinction
sedimentary rock	cast	fossil fuel
deposition		

Look for answers to these questions.

What are landforms?

What are weathering and erosion?

How can weathering and erosion form canyons?

How does deposition cause deltas and sand dunes?

How is sedimentary rock formed?

How are fossils formed?

What can fossils tell us about organisms of the past?

How do organisms of the past compare to organisms today?

How can fossils tell us about Earth's history?

What happens when organisms do not become fossils?

What are landforms?

You may not notice, but Earth's surface is changing all the time. What is Earth's surface, exactly? It's the tops of mountains and the bottoms of oceans. It's the sand on the beaches and the stones that break off boulders and rocks.

Over thousands and millions of years, Earth's surface undergoes processes that make and shape natural features called landforms. Mountains, valleys, hills, cliffs, and plains are all landforms that have been shaped by moving water, wind, and ice. These processes both build up and tear down land. But water, wind, and ice can do even more than that. They can help create a lasting record of Earth's history. Let's explore the ways that Earth's surface can change and also teach us about the past.

Formations such as this rock arch are the result of wind and water wearing away at rock over thousands of years.

The face of this rock has been weathered by a glacier moving over its surface.

What are weathering and erosion?

Weathering is the breaking down of rock into smaller pieces. Water, wind, and ice are the main agents of weathering.

You may have seen rock break apart. Over a long winter, water gets into cracks in rock. The water breaks the rock apart when it freezes.

Weathering occurs in other ways. Water can wash over rock and after a long time, wear the rock away. Wind can carry sand that wears rock away. Ice can also wear away rock. When a glacier moves over rock, it can wear it away and even break it apart. Chemicals can cause rock to crumble, and tree roots can break rock apart as the roots grow. The process of weathering is natural, and it accounts for Earth's constantly changing landforms.

Erosion is the process of moving weathered rock from one place to another. When Earth materials are broken apart or worn down, the pieces of rock move from one place to another. Water from melting snow rushing down a mountain is one way that weathering leads to erosion. The water washes away sand and other very small bits of rock, which are called sediment. The weathered materials are dropped or deposited in new locations in a process called deposition.

Over time, beaches face a lot of weathering and erosion. The waves beat against the shoreline, breaking up rock into smaller pieces and washing it away. The material erodes. There is less shoreline than before.

The process of erosion carries beach materials to new locations.

How can weathering and erosion form canyons?

Some landforms are caused by weathering and erosion. A canyon is a deep gorge, or cut, between cliffs of rock. A canyon can be caused by a river over a long period of time. The river forms sediment as it weathers the rock of the riverbed. The river picks up the sediment as it flows. The sediment scrapes more rock from the sides and bottom of the riverbed. The gorge gradually becomes deeper and deeper. Eventually, the gorge is so deep that a canyon is formed.

The constant movement of rushing river water can cause weathering and erosion of the riverbed.

Canyons may be large or small, and they can take a long time to form. One of the largest canyons, the Grand Canyon in Arizona, was formed by the Colorado River. It is up to 1.6 kilometers (1 mile) deep and 29 kilometers (18 miles) wide at some points. If you flew high over the canyon and looked down, the Colorado River would look tiny by comparison. It took millions of years to form a canyon so wide and deep.

Ice and wind may also help to form canyons through weathering and erosion.

The movement of the river over millions of years carved the Grand Canyon.

However, it's the movement of water, such as flowing rivers, that is the main cause of canyon formation.

This river delta was formed by the deposition of sediment that was washed down a river as the water made its way to the ocean.

How does deposition cause deltas and sand dunes?

You may wonder where all of the materials that wash away in the formation of a canyon end up. Sand, silt, and other sediment is carried along by a river. The sediment is moved along by the river until it is finally deposited at the mouth, or end, of the river. The mouth of a river is usually where the river meets the ocean. The river water flows into the ocean, but the sediment collects at the mouth of the river, building up to form a delta. A delta is a low, flat area of land that is built from sediment that was carried downstream by a river.

Another landform that is caused by deposition is a sand dune. A sand dune is a large deposit of sand that has been moved by the wind. Sand dunes form at beaches and in deserts, because these are areas where there is a lot of sand and wind that can carry and deposit it. Windstorms can occur frequently on beaches and in deserts, acting like giant brooms to push mounds of sand together into a hilly formation. Wind sweeps and lifts sand up one side of the dune. Gravity causes the sand to fall down the other side.

Sand dunes are the most constantly changing landforms. They can form very quickly, but wind does not work quickly on all objects. For example, over long periods of time, wind causes tiny particles of rock to break away, changing the shape of the rock in a very slow process.

The size and shape of sand dunes in the desert change often due to windstorms.

How is sedimentary rock formed?

The processes of weathering, erosion, and deposition do more than make and shape landforms. They also actually help to form layers of rock that can tell us about Earth's history. When rock is weathered and broken into smaller pieces, the sediment is carried away and deposited. Wind, water, ice, and gravity each play a role in moving the sediment and depositing it somewhere. Even after the sediment settles, it has not finished changing. A different and very slow process begins that forms layers of rock called sedimentary rock. The layers look like stripes in different shades. Each of these layers provides information about Earth's history.

Each layer of rock that you see was formed at a different time.

Every layer of sedimentary rock forms on top of the layer below it.

Once a layer of sediment has been deposited in a certain place, weight squeezes the particles together. Then more and more sediment is deposited on top of each layer. This buildup puts extra weight on each pile below it. Water is pushed out of sediment from the pressure and weight. Eventually, dissolved minerals get deposited in the spaces between the sediments. These dissolved minerals act like a glue that binds the sediments together. Over millions of years, pressure turns this tightly packed sediment to rock.

The color of the sediment in each rock layer is slightly different in each time period. This is because the minerals in the sediment on Earth's surface are different at different times in history.

How are fossils formed?

Scientists can find out a lot of information about Earth by looking at different layers of sedimentary rock. For instance, they can tell that the lower layers of rock were formed millions of years earlier than the higher layers of rock. They can even find fossils in the rock layers. A fossil is the remains or traces of a plant or an animal that lived long ago.

Fossils can be formed in different ways. A mold is an impression of an organism formed when sediment hardens around the organism's remains. The remains decay or dissolve, leaving a hollow area. This process forms an imprint. Suppose a shell leaves an imprint in sediment. After the sediment hardens, the shell may dissolve, leaving behind a hollow area shaped like the shell.

Paleontologists uncover and study fossils that have formed in layers of sedimentary rock.

A mold is an impression in sediment, while a cast is a model that forms out of sediment.

A cast is a model of an organism that's formed when sediment fills a mold and hardens. It takes a long time for a cast fossil to form. The sediment and minerals build up slowly inside a mold in order to form a cast.

Because living things decay, most organisms don't become fossils. They must die in or near water, which is where sediment is found. They must also be quickly covered by sediment. Most animal fossils are hard body parts, such as bones, because the soft parts of animals decay.

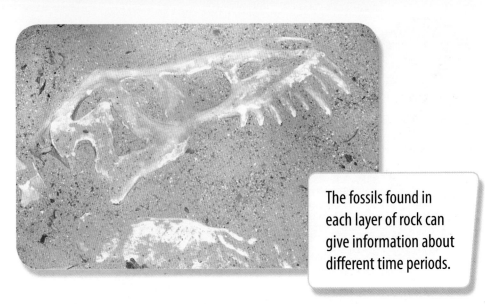

The fossils found in each layer of rock can give information about different time periods.

What can fossils tell us about organisms of the past?

Because fossils represent organisms that lived many thousands to many millions of years ago, they provide scientists with information about the past. All of the fossils in one layer of rock, for instance, give information about that layer's history, including the history of the organisms that lived at the time. Scientists use various methods to date rock layers in order to pinpoint the age of each layer of rock.

Scientists have been able to uncover fossils from very low layers of sedimentary rock. This has been possible because Earth's layers often shift to new positions. Over time, layers can tilt and be pushed up by the actions of earthquakes and other movements of Earth's plates.

Fossils can tell scientists what animals of the past looked like. They can also tell scientists what the animals ate and how they behaved. This information can't be determined from just one or two fossils, though. Fossils are like parts of a jigsaw puzzle. Large animals have to be pieced together from not only the parts that have been found

Index fossils can help scientists identify the age at which a rock layer was formed.

but also on *where* they were found. For example, scientists know when trees that produce seeds in cones first appeared on Earth. If they find the fossil of an animal in a rock layer from this same time, they have one clue to something the animal might have eaten.

Index fossils are the remains of common organisms that lived during a relatively short period in Earth's past. These organisms, such as trilobites, were widespread and existed in large numbers. Index fossils help scientists date rock layers.

How do organisms of the past compare to organisms today?

Scientists can also compare animals of the past to animals that live today. They can compare modern birds to the fossils of dinosaurs that flew. The comparisons can provide information about how animals have changed over millions of years.

When scientists find the fossil of an entire organism, they may be able to put the bones together to form a model. This can show what the organism's skeleton looked like. Comparing the parts of the skeleton to those of similar animals today can show how organisms have changed over time. For example, a fish's jaw size or a mammal's limb lengths can give information about changes to organisms.

This fossil shows that ancient shrimp were very similar to today's shrimp.

Scientists also use trace fossils to learn about animals that lived in the past. A trace fossil is not an actual body part of an organism, such as a bone. Instead, it is evidence of how an organism lived or behaved. A footprint in a stone can be a trace fossil. The marks an animal leaves after burrowing can be a trace fossil. The animal itself is not preserved, but traces of its life are left behind as clues to how the organism lived. These clues can be used to help scientists piece together information about the past. From trace fossils, scientists can learn where animals roamed, whether they roamed together or alone, and which of today's animals they may be most like.

Scientists study trace fossils to gather clues about how animals behaved.

What can fossils tell us about Earth's history?

Earth's history is long and rich. The layers of fossils that scientists uncover can show when big changes on Earth occurred. The fossil record shows that some dry land today was once an underwater home to many fish. Fossils of aquatic organisms can even be found on high mountaintops today. Fossils of trees are often found in places where there are no trees today. These hints give scientists a glimpse into Earth's past.

Fossil discoveries help scientists put together a timeline for the planet's history. Often, similar fossils from the same time period are found in places that are very far apart. These discoveries help support scientists' hypothesis that the continents were once connected and have moved slowly apart over time.

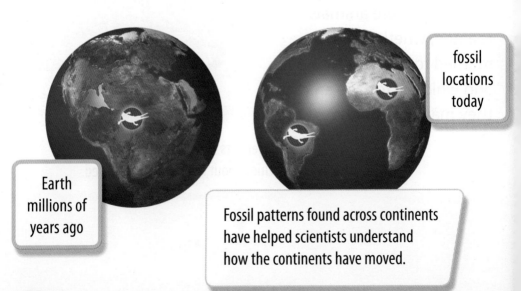

fossil locations today

Earth millions of years ago

Fossil patterns found across continents have helped scientists understand how the continents have moved.

A **mass extinction** is a period in which a large number of species disappear. Scientists look for evidence that might explain the cause. Volcanic ash deposited in sedimentary rock from a mass extinction may be evidence that a huge volcanic eruption occurred. Volcanic eruptions send ash and dust into the atmosphere, cutting off some of the sun's rays. Climate change results, and many species that cannot handle the change die off. Perhaps plant species die off first. Then animals, with no food source to rely on, die out.

Impacts by large asteroids can also be the cause of some mass extinctions. Asteroid impacts could cause severe climate changes, shifting the balance of life on Earth.

A large object from space can send huge amounts of dust into the air when it crashes into Earth, blocking sunlight for all living things. One asteroid that hit Earth was 16 kilometers (10 miles) across.

What happens when organisms do not become fossils?

The remains of most living things decompose and do not turn into fossils. The remains of some organisms may go through chemical changes, however. These chemical changes may result in fossil fuels. A fossil fuel is a natural energy source, such as oil or natural gas, that has formed from the remains of once-living things.

For example, coal forms from dead plants. Sediment covers plants that have fallen to the bottom of a lake or pond. Pressure is added with more layers of sediment. Temperatures also rise. The remains of the plants turn into a material called peat. The peat continues to be pressed and heated. Over millions of years, coal finally forms. Coal is taken from the ground and used as fuel to heat homes and businesses.

Temperature and pressure cause peat to form. More pressure and heat over a long period of time cause coal to form.

Coal is an important energy source, but the supply is limited. Peat bogs are places where coal is being formed right now. However, it will be a very long time before the peat in today's bogs becomes coal.

Oil and natural gas are also fossil fuels that take a long time to form under pressure and layers of sediment. They are made from tiny sea organisms, such as diatoms, that died millions of years ago. Pumps remove the oil and natural gas from beneath the ground so that they can be used as fuels.

Oil and natural gas take millions of years to form. Pumps bring the fossil fuels to the surface to be burned as fuels.

Earth's surface is constantly changing. Because of the processes of weathering, erosion, and deposition, Earth's surface will continue to change in the years to come.

Make Fossil Models

Use clay and hard objects such as shells to make models of a cast and a mold fossil. Exchange models with a partner and identify each model as either a cast or a mold.

Write a Report

Summarize how the processes of weathering and erosion take place and what kinds of landforms result from these changes to Earth's surface.

Glossary

cast [KAST] A model of an organism, formed when sediment fills a mold and hardens.

deposition [dep·uh·ZISH·uhn] The dropping or settling of eroded materials.

erosion [ih·ROH·zhuhn] The process of moving sediment from one place to another.

fossil [FAHS·uhl] The remains or traces of a plant or an animal that lived long ago.

fossil fuel [FAHS·uhl FYOO·uhl] Fuel, such as coal, oil, and natural gas, formed from the remains of once-living things.

index fossil [IN·deks FAHS·uhl] A fossil of a type of organism that lived in many places during a relatively short time span.

mass extinction [MAS ek·STINGK·shuhn] A period in which a large number of species become extinct.

mold [MOHLD] An impression of an organism, formed when sediment hardens around the organism.

sedimentary rock [SED·uh·MEN·tuh·ree RAHK] A type of rock that forms when layers of sediment are pressed together.

weathering [WETH·er·ing] The breaking down of rocks on Earth's surface into smaller pieces.